The False Laws of Narrative
The Poetry of Fred Wah

The False Laws of Narrative
The Poetry of Fred Wah

Selected
with an
introduction by
Louis Cabri
and an
afterword by
Fred Wah

lps
LAURIER POETRY SERIES

Wilfrid Laurier University Press
[WLU]

We acknowledge the support of the Canada Council for the Arts for our publishing program. We acknowledge the financial support of the Government of Canada through the Book Publishing Industry Development Program for our publishing activities.

Library and Archives Canada Cataloguing in Publication

Wah, Fred, 1939–
[Poems. Selections]
    The false laws of narrative : the poetry of Fred Wah / selected, with an introduction, by Louis Cabri.

(Laurier poetry series)
Includes biographical references.
Issued also in electronic format.
ISBN 978-1-55458-046-0

    I. Cabri, Louis   II. Title.   III. Title: Poems. Selections.   IV. Series: Laurier poetry series

PS8545.A28A6 2009   C811'.54   C2009-904031-X

Library and Archives Canada Cataloguing in Publication

Wah, Fred, 1939–
[Poems. Selections]
    The false laws of narrative [electronic resource] : the poetry of Fred Wah / selected, with an introduction, by Louis Cabri.

(Laurier poetry series)
Includes biographical references.
Electronic edited collection in PDF, ePub, and XML formats.
Issued also in print format.
ISBN 978-1-55458-162-7

    I. Cabri, Louis   II. Title.   III. Title: Poems. Selections.   IV. Series: Laurier poetry series

PS8545.A28A6 2009   C811'.54

© 2009 Wilfrid Laurier University Press
Waterloo, Ontario N2L 3C5, Canada
www.wlupress.wlu.ca

Cover image by Xu Bing: *The Living Word* (carved, painted acrylic characters, nylon monofilament), 2001. Courtesy Xu Bing Studio and Sotheby's New York.
Cover design and text design by P.J. Woodland.

This book is printed on FSC recycled paper and is certified Ecologo. It is made from 100% post-consumer fibre, processed chlorine free, and manufactured using biogas energy.

Printed in Canada

Table of Contents

Foreword

At the beginning of the twenty-first century, poetry in Canada—writing and publishing it, reading and thinking about it—finds itself in a strangely conflicted place. We have many strong poets continuing to produce exciting new work, and there is still a small audience for poetry; but increasingly, poetry is becoming a vulnerable art, for reasons that don't need to be rehearsed.

But there are things to be done: we need more real engagement with our poets. There needs to be more access to their work in more venues—in classrooms, in the public arena, in the media—and there need to be more, and more different kinds, of publications that make the wide range of our contemporary poetry more widely available.

The hope that animates this series from Wilfrid Laurier University Press is that these volumes help to create and sustain the larger readership that contemporary Canadian poetry so richly deserves. Like our fiction writers, our poets are much celebrated abroad; they should just as properly be better known at home.

Our idea is to ask a critic (sometimes herself a poet) to select thirty-five poems from across a poet's career; write an engaging, accessible introduction; and have the poet write an afterword. In this way, we think that the usual practice of teaching a poet through eight or twelve poems from an anthology is much improved upon; and readers in and out of classrooms will have more useful, engaging, and comprehensive introductions to a poet's work. Readers might also come to see more readily, we hope, the connections among, as well as the distances between, the life and the work.

It was the ending of an Al Purdy poem that gave Margaret Laurence the epigraph for *The Diviners*: "but they had their being once / and left a place to stand on." Our poets still do, and they are leaving many places to stand on. We hope that this series helps, variously, to show how and why this is so.

—*Neil Besner*
General Editor

Biographical Note

Fred Wah was born in Swift Current, Saskatchewan, in 1939, and grew up in the Nelson area of British Columbia. His parents were owners and operators of several Chinese-Canadian cafés. In 1962 he married Pauline Butling and graduated with a B.A. in English and Music from the University of British Columbia. As an undergraduate, Wah co-founded *Tish: A Poetry Newsletter, Vancouver* (1961–63) and attended courses by visiting U.S. poets Charles Olson and Robert Creeley. Wah studied with Creeley at the University of New Mexico, where he founded *Sum* magazine, then with Olson at SUNY–Buffalo, where he graduated with an M.A. in Linguistics and Literature in 1967. During these years, Wah published his first books of poetry (*Lardeau* and *Mountain*); became contributing editor to *Niagara Frontier Review* (1964–66), *The Magazine of Further Studies* (1965–69), and *Open Letter: A Canadian Journal of Writing and Theory* (1965–present); and was among sixteen poets in Raymond Souster's *New Wave Canada: The New Explosion in Canadian Poetry* (1966). Wah returned in 1967 to the Nelson area of B.C., edited and published *Scree* magazine, and taught at Selkirk College and the David Thompson University Centre. He inaugurated DTUC's creative writing program, attracting young poets, many of whom went on to found Vancouver's Kootenay School of Writing. While living in the Nelson area, Wah published over ten poetry books, including *Loki Is Buried at Smoky Creek: Selected Poems* (1980), edited by George Bowering, and *Waiting for Saskatchewan*, which won the 1985 Governor General's Award for Poetry. Wah moved to Calgary in 1989 and taught at the University of Calgary until his retirement in 2003. Among his numerous publications are the poetry book *So Far* (1991), which won the Stephan G. Stephansson Award; the biofiction *Diamond Grill* (1996), which received the Howard O'Hagan Award for Short Fiction; and *Faking It: Poetics and Hybridity, Critical Writing 1984–1999* (2000), which won the Gabrielle Roy Prize for Literary Criticism in English Canada. Wah currently splits his time between the Kootenays and Vancouver, and continues to write. Two recent collections are *Sentenced to Light* (2008), text-based collaborations with visual artists, and *is a door* (2009).

The False Laws of Narrative: Fred Wah's Poetics

"[P]oetry today takes on the colour of a relational utterance."
—Fred Wah, *Tish* 4 (1961)[1]

1. Grand Collage Epic and Proprioceptive Lyric: Two Paradigms

In a 2007 talk about the poetry that was formative to his development, Fred Wah approaches his topic by outlining paradigms for modern lyric and epic, "paradigm" meaning model, pattern, or example of poetic form.[2] His exemplary paradigm for modern lyric is William Carlos Williams's 1954 poem "The Desert Music," and for modern epic, a technique, collage—the juxtaposing of texts, images, materials from different times and places and media.

Wah learned first-hand about collage in poetry from west-coast USAmerican poet Robert Duncan, who had been invited starting in 1959 to give to young Vancouver poets a series of informal talks on poetry that mattered to him. Duncan gave an account of the modernist revolution in poetic forms in a way that changed their poetry lives.[3]

The great upstart *Tish* newsletter—the name has come to identify a formation of poets—resulted from Duncan's visits. Wah was co-founder. The *Tish* poets picked up where poet-editors Louis Dudek in Montreal and Raymond Souster in Toronto left off—continuing the turn away from British paradigms of rhythm, rhyme, reason, toward free-verse American paradigms like those inspired by collage techniques and like Williams's as found in, for instance, Diane Di Prima's and LeRoi Jones's *The Floating Bear* and other underground (as they were then rightly called) poetry newsletters and magazines. The idea of *Tish* would stir up controversy among Canadian cultural nationalists even though Fred Wah and other poets associated with *Tish* (including George Bowering and Daphne Marlatt) were articulating Canada's western cultural geography in their writing and even though most Canadian verse was still largely beholden to British paradigms of poetic form. Many of Wah's poems inspired by USAmerican paradigms enact events and conditions specific to the west coast and mountainous interior of British

Columbia, such as "Gold Hill" (prospecting), "Hamill's Last Stand" (logging), and "Chain" (surveying), all included here.

Modern poets who use the collage technique often aspire to lift details from different contexts to form a cultural whole. Duncan, for example, wanted "a poetry of all poetries, grand collage" (*Bending the Bow*, vii), epic in dimensions, that can let—hauntingly so—"all of the old stories / whisper once more," as he puts it in one poem (*The Opening of the Field*, 68). By "old stories," Duncan mostly means ancient Greek, Hebrew, Egyptian, and Christian myths. The question is whether such myths can help to tell a contemporary story. Duncan believed so[4]—as did many modernist writers. Judging from Wah's poetry, Wah does not. Wah's poetry disentangles itself from modernist ambitions of representing a "grand collage" of "old stories" based on a cultures-of-the-world unity. For example, the collage-like diary sequence, "Hermes Poems," from *So Far* (1991), thinks of itself as "a kind of samskara to scare out the europe ghosts," and therefore as not merely wry commentary on the everyday commerce involved in any contemporary reproduction of a classical figure such as Hermes (commentary such as one finds in Pound and Joyce). However, the mythmaking that underlies aboriginal oral telling is a different matter, a present-day difference that Wah acknowledges (Duncan, curiously, overlooks aboriginal myths). "Akokli (goat) creek," for example, is the title of a poem from Wah's first book, *Lardeau* (1965). One way its parentheses function is to suggest that the word *goat* is a direct translation of the Ktunaxa word *akokli*, but *akokli* apparently means horn or antler, not goat.[5] In other words, Wah's title parallels, but does not unite and conflate, two linguistic worlds and their cultural histories, Western and aboriginal. The language of Wah's title points to conflicting claims that exist even at the level of the name for a creek and mountain in the Kootenay Lake district of B.C. A similar cultural parallelism operates in *Pictograms from the Interior of B.C.* (1975), from which I've selected three poems together with reproductions of the aboriginal rock paintings that accompanied them in that volume. Wah's untitled poem beginning "September spawn" responds to the illustration of a Ktunaxa Nation rock painting located at Procter, B.C.[6] The poem does not pretend to represent an authentic translation of the rock art that possibly dates from 200–300 years ago. Wah approaches the pictographic shapes and their uncertain meanings in a playfully improvisational mode that is fully aware of its contemporaneity, which is a way of writing I shall explore here as central to his poetics.[7]

For his "grand collage," Duncan was thinking of Ezra Pound's *Cantos* ("songs"), which went so wide as to incorporate twenty-odd languages for "old stories" from Europe and Asia. Pound even had his own name for writing by collage—"the ideogrammic method"—in homage to the Chinese written character whose style he loved. The *Cantos* invest in a long-standing European fantasy that the look of a Chinese written character resembles what it refers to—which misconstrues how any language largely works, but paradoxically founds English-language modernism (paradoxically so, because, according to Pound's Imagist manifestos,[8] the hard-edged "real" image of an Imagist poem—such as by Hilda Doolittle ["H. D."]—opposes fantasy).[9]

Wah's differences from Pound's ideogrammic legacy for poetry become perceptible by contrasting *Waiting for Saskatchewan*—Wah was born in Swift Current, Saskatchewan—with Andrew Suknaski's *Silk Trail*, both published in 1985. What Wah says in his 2007 talk about modern epic and lyric paradigms helps to differentiate between these two poetry sequences that implicitly share as their common theme the collective hardships experienced by Chinese emigrants to Canada. These hardships included a systemic racism that narrowly prescribed job and most other social opportunities, a prohibitive immigration tax, extremely restrictive federal immigration policies,[10] and no voting rights. Suknaski's *Silk Trail* follows Pound's epic paradigm by collaging texts—either through citation, paraphrase, or allusion—as disparate as official CPR and federal government letters about labour and race relations, and Ma Huan's fifteenth-century travelogue. But instead of such epic history-telling, which for Suknaski excludes a first-person narrator,[11] Wah favours a lyric paradigm and in particular what a lyric paradigm can offer a search for missing personal history. The diary mode of the lyric paradigm organizes the beginning of "Aug 5" (included in this selection), which opens: "We tour Hong Kong today in a bus with a guide hyping photos of ourselves. I start taking notes re places I've seen my father since he died." In these lines, the centuries-old Western fantasy of "the Orient" as projecting the West's own repressed desires becomes ironized in the person of a tour guide "hyping photos of ourselves."[12] Homogenizing stereotypes of "Chineseness"—whether concerning China's languages or its peoples—are also acknowledged here as having been internalized (he sees his father everywhere).[13] Use of a lyric paradigm allows the poet to disclose personal observations such as these, whose meanings are unfolded in the process of being worked out, not with finality.

Wah found an alternative to Pound's example of epic-like collage in Charles Olson's poetry. Olson identified literature, capital "l," with the immediate act of writing. At the same time, Olson went, historically, "from Homer back" (*A Bibliography on America*, 40) to a time before the ancient Greek "beginnings" of Western civilization. Olson thus offered a critique of Western ethnocentrism. Except Olson also went all the way back to

"Pleistocene man," the epoch during which *Homo sapiens* emerged, 300,000–400,000 years ago. The Pleistocene is "almost like poetry," Olson marvels, because from it "you can learn the language of being alive [...] as though you were learning to read and write for the first time" (*Pleistocene Man,* 9). In other words, the Pleistocene is still with us, hidden in our body's autonomic nervous system, to be reawakened by writing. Olson's epic collage of prehistoric past and postmodern present imagines *writing and living in the human body as if for the first time.* Every body carries in itself—everybody carries in her- or himself that distinctive Pleistocene species-difference: being-alive.

Olson's poetry and poetics greatly appealed to Wah for many reasons, not least because Olson tried to get out of what he called "the Western box" of assumptions about the world, such as assumptions governing the Self's relations to (and with) the Other. As John Clarke puts it: "At the collapse of the Minoan civilization and the beginning of the 'Europan', the *Other* was dispersed *elsewhere*, the antithetical contours of which would not be felt until after the 'discovery' of the New World" (151). In practical terms, Olson helped Wah write from a lyric paradigm by reinforcing the importance of William Carlos Williams's example. For as Wah says in his Windsor talk, Williams proposed, as did Olson after him, that poetry be written from the "fragmented attentions of the grounded, fixed, actual" of the poet's own lived world. Wah's world included, he tells us in his talk, summers shoring-up B.C.-interior trails with the loose stone called riprap. No wonder the word *riprap* attracted Wah's attention when he found it in Gary Snyder's lines: "Lay down these words / Before your mind like rocks // [... like the] riprap of things" (Snyder, 30). Instead of a grand-collage sweep through histories, myths, and languages of the world, as in a Duncan or Pound, USAmerican poet Gary Snyder's 1959 poem "Riprap," from which his lines are taken, declared to Wah that writing can issue from common and local knowledge. So, as had Snyder and Olson, Wah turned to Williams's lyrical paradigm for how to lay riprap in a poem, how to *enact* riprap and not just thematize it. How, as Williams distinguishes it,

> – to place myself (in
> my nature) beside nature

> – to imitate
> nature (for to copy nature would be a
> shameful thing) (*Collected Poems II,* 276)

Williams's instruction to poets, in these lines, is not to copy nature at one remove (doing so would emphasize nature's separateness and stark differences from the human world). Rather, the poet's task, as Williams says elsewhere, is "the perfection of new forms as *additions* to nature" (*Collected Poems I*, 226; my emphasis). The poet should let words "place" her inside the unique experience of being-alive, inside the poet's *own* nature, in and behind processes of perception that are visual, emotional, verbal, so these individuated processes can be imitated, and Nature, thereby, added to. Another of Olson's key ideas crucially elaborates Williams's point: "one's life is informed from and by one's own literal body" (*A Bibiliography on America*, 18). One's own "literal body" informs one's life, however not, paradoxically, in a literal way. Writing must go after "the DEPTH implicit in physical being—built-in space-time specifics" (18), specifics Olson characterized physiologically as proprioceptive.[14] And for Wah, even the body's cells contain memories of one's life (and of one's genealogy): poetry is a "histograph," a tissue of cells, he metaphorically says in poem 50 of *Music at the Heart of Thinking*, encoded with the forgotten and/or repressed past. For writing to get at the past buried in the living body of the writer, writing must necessarily declare the prevailing laws of narrative—and the narratives themselves—to be false, incomplete.

Following Olson's proprioceptive call to (and following Williams's call to) imitate nature by way of writing from the built-in space-time specifics of one's given body, Wah's poetry emerges from a lyric paradigm, but one that radically qualifies what is conventionally meant by "lyric." By locating in and behind processes of perception, a proprioceptive act of writing paradoxically decentres and demotes the "self" in "self-expression," the meaning-full "I" in language. Writing may start from coordinates located anywhere else in the body's perceptual field other than in the ego's "I." Writing need not, in fact for Olson should not, begin from the coordinates of this reasoning abtraction. Writing could begin instead with the mouth positioning lip and tongue to shape sound-patterns (i.e., language) out of the body's breath-rhythm.

The riprap of Wah's poetry learns from the grand collage epic, but takes off with the proprioceptive lyric. His riprap offers the juxtapositional openness and loose-endedness of collage, without collage's grand-historical, presumptive scale. Wah's riprap offers lyricism—without lyricism's I-centric, i-dentical iteration of poetic voice.

2. An Improvisational Paradigm for Poetry

I've suggested above that Fred Wah's poetics involves enacting embodied perceptual processes in language. One way he does that is through sound. "[W]hat one 'means' is not primary, or central to what the po-em *is*" (Open letter, 24), he once wrote in an open letter to Jewish American poet Louis Zukofsky, searching for a way to understand Zukofsky's musicality.[15] Wah is paraphrasing a line by Archibald MacLeish, that "a poem must not mean but be."[16] MacLeish's line continues to serve as a pedagogical touchstone for handling that difficult thing, the modern poem. But notice the hyphen in Wah's spelling: "po-em." Adding a hyphen transforms MacLeish's line, in that Wah's paraphrase no longer asserts the poem be thought of *spatially* only— the modernist poem as difficult *thing*, an object that just "is." By hyphenating the word "poem" as "po-em," Wah reminds readers that, uttered, a word is made of syllables—"po," "em"—in temporal succession. Continues Wah: "[I]t is the 'working' within, whatever form, that interests me." "Working" entails an act, such as placing a hyphen inside the form of a word, so that readers notice how words are made so that sounds "never stop changing places" over the alphabet's twenty-six graphic letters.

The direction Wah takes the Olson–Williams paradigm of "locating in" perceptual processes is toward working with writing as sound-elements in time—sound that turns away from traditional British prosodic measure and beat and listens instead to American jazz improvisation:

> the words don't come from other worlds
> each is a time sign
>
> remembers itself only once
> between all other words [*So Far*, 47]

These lines state a paradox of jazz music's improvisational method. The paradox involves understanding time. If a sequence of words is *literally* a "time sign," a sign of time passing, then that sequence, that sign, exists only once in the present, for the duration of its utterance alone, and no other words can recapture its unique movement through time again. That's a paradox—a "time sign" that cannot reflect on the passage of time!

With the poem-excerpt above, Wah asks readers to imagine a scenario where they are reading the poem *as the poet is writing it,* and to imagine that the total structure and vocabulary of the poem shifts with every new word the poet adds. A time sign that "remembers" itself *only once* is like a musical note in a jazz performance that is played not by following a score (the same note sequence every time the score is played) but by improvising within the music's structured moment. A word need remember only once (on the poet's behalf) its own act of placement in the poetic design, because the design itself is part of an ongoing improvisational process that changes the design as it goes (but there is always, of course, a design—the improvisational moment does not occur freely, out of nowhere).[17]

I take the phrase "time sign" to be Wah's declaration of his own poetic paradigm. A "time sign" for the nonce ("nonce" means for the one time only), embraces the accidental and the contingent in an improvisational moment at the heart of the writing process. A poem like this one (in the excerpt, above) theorizes its act *as* it acts. Wah calls such a poem a "theom," his word-blend of "theory" and "poem." Wah writes many theoms. Wah's paradoxical "time sign" tries to lift airborne on pulmonary winds, float on heartbeat cycles over the glottal chasm where breath begins and ends, and like jazz trace sound-patterns—cell memory—moment to moment.

3. Working within Wah's Meaning and Sound

Wah's time-sign paradigm of embodied sound is found in his ongoing prose-poem sequence, *Music at the Heart of Thinking*. I'm going to carefully examine No. 94. The elements of this poem echo in varied ways throughout Wah's poetry, including this sequence, from which nine poems have been selected for this volume. Semantically it might be helpful to think of the following poem as made of two sets of terms for nature, each containing contrasts. The first set of contrasting terms in the poem imagines nature via *spatial* metaphors: a "gardened world" contrasts with a nature-wild world of "slope of scree and marmot whistle." The second set builds *temporal* metaphors for nature by contrasting improvisational with (what might be called and will be explained below) ratiocinative ways of writing. Based on this poem, I've associated the writing act with time (the utterance's temporal dimension), not with space (the page's spatial layout of words), which generally holds true for Wah's poetry.[18] Notice also how the writing act itself forms part of what the poem is about: No. 94 is a theom. Unlike improvisational writing, ratiocinative writing aims at achieving, in the words of the poem, a "mass synapse" effect, which I take to mean that ratiocinative writing builds a unifying coherence from its unfolding argument, so that, at poem's end, it is as if all synapses in the brain fire at once in one coherent illumination of meaning. By contrast, the improvisational way of writing is to proceed haphazardly by leaps in the moment—like neurons firing in the dark over synaptic junctions—from one noun and prepositional phrase to another, the poet freely associating, forming what linguists call garden-path sentences (sentences that do not follow a narrow and linear path). In improvisational writing, the poet aims to get lost in the moment's act of writing, and be guided by what in the language is found there—this is Wah's paradigm of the time sign. In ratiocinative writing, by contrast, the poet wants the writing to knowingly lead somewhere—to a conclusion that preferably includes knowledge (self-knowledge as well).

Listen for the sounds as they change places over the letters of the poem:

> This is no mass synapse I'm after and I've known awhile now being
> lost is as simple as sitting on a log but the fumble jerked mystique

clouds grabbing as the staked mistake or stacked and treasured garbage
belongs familiar to a gardened world disturbed as heat.

O soft anxiousness to be found again and again estranged but
marvelous then enlived slope of scree and marmot whistle so that
synchronous foreignicity rages in music I want to put into a region
of the cadence before falling's recognized you know

where there's that disgraceful ensoulment Mao called swimming.
[*Alley* 38]

As in many of Wah's poems, this poem outlines two opposing space-time
coordinates from which to plot—from which to write—"being alive." The poem
negatively characterizes space-time coordinates plotted from "a gardened world"
(plotted along the spatial axis) and ratiocinative writing-as-"mass synapse"
(plotted along the temporal axis). But the poem *positively* characterizes space-
time coordinates plotted from wild nature ("scree and marmot whistle") and
improvisational writing-as-synaptic-leap. The axes formed by wild nature
(space) and improvisational synaptic leaps (time) produce writing as if in a state
of nature free of social construction—in other words, as if uncontaminated by
the layerings of history (personal and otherwise). In such a state of nature, the
body appears as if intact, proprioceptively writing itself "being alive." But as if in
a totally different universe, space-time coordinates that form along the spatial
axis by gardened nature and along the temporal by ratiocinative writing-as-
mass-synapse evoke an *opposite* condition. In the latter condition, nature itself
becomes a social construction (nature is a gardened, not a wild, world), and the
writing body compromised, burdened with history ("stacked and treasured
garbage"), a "disgraceful ensoulment."

Yet it would be a mistake to assume that Wah's poetic paradigm of
improvised "time signs" ultimately achieves, by using the positively-
characterized space-time coordinates I've just described, a state of pure
immediacy, of exclusively "wild human nature" in a thoroughly embodied
writing. In Wah's poetry, neither ratiocinative nor improvisational writing
mode wins out, since each needs to be opposed to the other in order for any
writing to get done. One set of space-time coordinates for living and writing
opposes the other set, creating a mutually-alienating effect—an effect of, as
the poem itself reflexively theorizes, "synchronous foreignicity," one of Wah's
key ideas in poetics. Wah's poetry traces the simultaneous conflict of writing
both improvisationally and ratiocinatively, both "for nature" and "for history."

The role negation plays in the poem helps to produce this dialectic between
mutually opposing positions. Improvisational writing-as-synaptic-leaps is not
positively affirmed but inferred via negation of the opposing way of writing:
"This is no mass synapse…." Ratiocinative writing-as-mass-synapse is also not

positively affirmed but inferred by negation of *its* opposing way of writing: "that disgraceful ensoulment Mao called swimming." This line may need a little explanation. Swimming, in itself, is a kind of natural improvisation (one might swim as one likes, for swimming's sake), but when identified with former Chinese communist leader Mao Zedong, swimming alludes to a historical event—foretold in Zedong's poem "Swimming"—of his building a bridge at Wuhan over the Yangtze River, memorializing his swim across it. Mao thus negates the improvisational act of swimming for swimming's sake by elevating it into a socially-symbolic, ratiocinative act of industrial modernization in China. And there is a second negation working this line as well, a negation of a negation, since Wah negatively characterizes what Zedong does, as "disgraceful ensoulment," as monumentalizing self-aggrandizement.

The poem's remarkable sound patterning reinforces these two mutually opposing space-time coordinates for living and writing. Two sounds are in "complementary distribution" (as a linguist might say) in the poem, meaning that where the one sound predominates in the poem, the other sound is minimized, and vice versa. The sounds in question refer to two ways to pronounce English vowels: nasalized (the *a* in *anxiousness*) or non-nasalized (the *a* in *bat*). Non-nasalized vowels predominate, by a factor greater than two, in the poem's first sentence (the poem's first paragraph forms one sentence). Nasalized vowels predominate, by a factor greater than two, in the poem's second sentence (the second and third stanzas of the poem).

If the poem offers a culminating moment of ratiocinative illumination, this will necessarily have to occur (because, remember that the writing act is associated with time) in the latter half of the poem—which is where nasalized vowels predominate. It happens that nasalization has something to do with being in a state of nature that is not yet entirely socialized. Nasal consonants are the first sounds a child articulates (the nasal *m* in *Mama* is articulated before the non-nasal *p* in *Papa*, according to Jakobson), and of course, childhood is within the lyric Romantic tradition closest to a state of nature preceding history. But here again is further evidence of the poem's paradoxical duality, since the culminating moment of illumination to be found in the poem (a coherent illumination which is associated with ratiocinative writing and with history) is *an argument for nature* (which is associated with improvisational writing). Many readers have noticed how Wah's poetry yearns for a return to something called home, and this poem arrives there—in sound.

Wah's poetry often induces a crisis in its own language. In this poem from *Music at the Heart of Thinking*, the crisis is one of falling in between two space-time coordinates for living and writing, and of being unable to free oneself decisively from the one so as to completely embrace the other. Neither the state of nature nor the inescapable and historical condition of living in society really offers that impossible ticket home. Both space-time coordinates for living and writing exist at the same time—in the poem. Home is, perhaps, the poem itself. Wah's writings improvise on this sometimes cruel condition of in-betweenness in many different ways. Notions of the hyphen—racial, cultural, and grammatical—permeate his writing as a result of how deeply this in-betweenness informs his poetics, a poetics whose outlines I've tried to mark out here.

Appendix: Oral and Nasal Vowel Distribution in Fred Wah's "Music at the Heart of Thinking 94"

Oral (the *a*-as-in-*bat* vowel only):

Sentence 1:   Sentence 2:

Para. 1	Para. 2	Para. 3
-ass	aux-	that
-apse	ag-	raw
aft-	that	
as	a	
grab		
that		
stack		

Nasal (all nasalized vowels, not only the *a*-as-in-*anxious* nasalized vowel):

Sentence 1:   Sentence 2:

Para. 1	Para. 2	Para. 3
known	anx-	en-
simple	found	swim-
on	-gain	-ming
fumble	-gain	
and	and	
and	ranged	
-longs	then	
	en-	
	marm-	
	syn-	
	in-	

Note: A vowel is called "oral" when to pronounce it air flows through the oral cavity of the mouth alone. Such a vowel becomes "nasalized" when in order to pronounce it air must flow through both oral and nasal passages. In many dialects of English, nasalization occurs to vowels sequenced before nasal consonants like *m* and *n*. That's what I've assumed here.

Notes

1 My epigraph is from Wah's essay "Margins into Lines: A Relationship."
2 Wah's talk, "Propped Forms—Ashes of Content," delivered as a Transparency Machine Event at the University of Windsor, 13 March 2007, is available in downloadable audio at http://web4.uwindsor.ca/english.
3 Wah recorded Duncan's Vancouver talks on the history of twentieth-century poetry. They are available at Slought Foundation, http://slought.org. See Pauline Butling and Frank Davey for first-hand accounts of Duncan's influence in Vancouver.
4 For Duncan's views about myth, see his essay "The Truth and Life of Myth."
5 For the meaning of *akokli*, the B.C. Geographical Names Index cites linguist Randy Bouchard, who in 1973 cites Mrs. Marcilene Manuel, from Nanaimo, a speaker of the endangered Ktunaxa language ("Akokli"). For more on the Ktunaxa language, see the FirstVoices project: http://www.firstvoices.com.
6 Wah's *Pictograms from the Interior of B.C.* includes information on the rock paintings that form the basis of the poems. The illustration accompanying Wah's poem beginning "We are different" is of an Interior Salish (Okanagan) rock painting at Mica Creek, B.C. The illustration for Wah's "nv s ble" is of a Ktunaxa Nation rock painting at Armstrong Bay, Washington.
7 Wah's relationship to "aboriginality" in its many modes—from Duncan's "old stories" to Jerome Rothenberg's "ethnopoetics," and from the literature of "ancient" China to the oral traditions of first peoples—strikes me as nuanced and complex. For instance, I perceive cultural parallelism and inauthenticity (i.e., a self-declared "faking it," leading to improvisation) in *Pictograms from the Interior of B.C.*, not a translation project in ethnopoetics. For a reading of the "linguistic unconscious" of Wah's book as part of the latter project, see Steve McCaffery.
8 For Pound's Imagist manifestos, see his "A Retrospect."
9 For more on this European fantasy about the Chinese language, see linguist John DeFrancis and intellectual historian Haun Saussy.
10 Canada's immigration policy was so "highly restrictive," historian Peter S. Li says, that "[t]he Chinese population in Canada decreased drastically between 1931 and 1951" (73).
11 In Aristotle's famous definition in his *Poetics*, epic is a genre that necessarily excludes a first-person narrator's experiences.
12 One can also read the irony of the line so that it is the "we," not the tour guide, who is "hyping photos of ourselves." For the groundbreaking account of how the East is a projection of the West's interests and desires, see Edward Said.

13 Anthony B. Chan astutely offers a context for understanding how complex are these processes of racialization when he writes: "Years of neglect, isolation and indifference had cut off North America's Asians, whose own roots were in the gold rush and railway-building days, from Asian tradition and culture. But white North America's insistence on associating Western-born Asians with a mythological Asia that existed only in their own minds fostered powerful stereotypes that, ironically, were absorbed even by Asians themselves" (188–89).

14 "Proprioception" is not a common word, but the idea behind Olson's use of the term has become an entire branch of study. Linguist Mark Johnson has developed the concept of "embodied cognition" in order to account for the intimate interrelationship between body and language. See, for example, his book (co-written with George Lakoff) *Philosophy in the Flesh.*

15 An excellent introduction to Zukofsky's poetry is the recent *Selected Poems,* edited by Charles Bernstein.

16 "Ars Poetica," a 1926 poem by Archibald MacLeish, whose title, from Horace, means art of poetry.

17 Poetic theories of improvisation are yet to be worked out. For an overview of musical theories of improvisation, see George E. Lewis.

18 Jeff Derksen corroborates this impression when he observes: "Fred Wah's work looks at the landscape to find time" (149).

Works Cited

"Akokli." BC Geographical Names Index. Government of BC homepage. 9 July 2008, http://ilmbwww.gov.bc.ca/bcgn-bin/bcg10?name=516.

Butling, Pauline. "Who Is She? Inside/Outside Literary Communities." In *Writing in Our Time: Canada's Radical Poetries in English (1957–2003).* Ed. Pauline Butling and Susan Rudy. Waterloo, ON: Wilfrid Laurier UP, 2005. 141–60.

Chan, Anthony B. *Gold Mountain: The Chinese in the New World.* Vancouver, BC: New Star, 1983.

Clarke, John. *From Feathers to Iron: A Concourse of World Poetics.* Santa Cruz, CA: Tombouctou Books, 1986.

Davey, Frank. "Introducing *Tish.*" In *The Writing Life: Historical and Critical Views of the Tish Movement.* Intr. Frank Davey. Ed. C.H. Gervais. Coatsworth, ON: Black Moss, 1976. 150–61.

DeFrancis, John. *The Chinese Language: Fact and Fantasy.* Honolulu: University of Hawai'i Press, 1984.

Derksen, Jeff. "Sites Taken as Signs: Place, the Open Text, and Enigma in New Vancouver Writing." In *Vancouver: Representing the Postmodern City.* Ed. Paul Delany. Vancouver: Talonbooks, 1993. 144–61.

Duncan, Robert. *Bending the Bow.* New York: New Directions, 1968.

———. "The Truth and Life of Myth." In *Fictive Certainties.* New York, NY: New Directions, 1998. 1–59.

————. "Vancouver 1961: Lecture #1" (23 July 1961); "Vancouver 1961: Lecture #2" (24 July 1961); "Vancouver 1961: Lecture #3" (25 July 1961). Slought Foundation, University of Pennsylvania, http://slought.org.

————. *The Opening of the Field*. New York: Grove Press/Evergreen, 1960.

FirstVoices. First Peoples' Cultural Foundation. 12 July 2008, http://www.firstvoices.com.

Jakobson, Roman. "Why 'Mama' and 'Papa'?" *On Language*. Ed. Linda Waugh and Monique Monville-Burston. Cambridge, MA: Harvard UP, 1990. 305–14.

Johnson, Mark, and George Lakoff. *Philosophy in the Flesh: The Embodied Mind and Its Challenge to Western Thought*. New York: Basic Books, 1999.

Lewis, George E. "Improvised Music after 1950: Afrological and Eurological Perspectives." *Black Music Research Journal* 22, Supplement (2002): 215–46.

Li, Peter S. *The Chinese in Canada*. 2nd ed. Don Mills, ON: Oxford UP, 1998.

MacLeish, Archibald. "Ars Poetica." *Collected Poems 1917–1982*. New York: Houghton Mifflin, 1985. 106.

McCaffery, Steve. "Anti-Phonies: Fred Wah's Pictograms from the Interior of B.C." *North of Intention: Critical Writings 1973–1986*. New York: Roof, 1986.

Olson, Charles. *Pleistocene Man*. Buffalo, NY: Institute of Further Studies, 1968.

————. *A Bibliography on America, Proprioception & Other Notes & Essays*. Bolinas, CA: Four Seasons Foundation, 1974.

Pound, Ezra. "A Retrospect." *Literary Essays of Ezra Pound*. Ed. and intr. T.S. Eliot. London: Faber and Faber, 1960. 3–14.

————. *The Cantos of Ezra Pound*. New York: New Directions, 1996.

Said, Edward W. *Orientalism*. New York: Vintage, 1979.

Saussy, Haun. "The Prestige of Writing: Wen^2, Letter, Picture, Image, Ideography." *Sino-Platonic Papers* 75 (February 1997). Department of East Asian Languages and Civilizations, University of Pennsylvania. 10 December 2008, http://www.sino-platonic.org.

Snyder, Gary. *Riprap, & Cold Mountain Poems*. San Francisco: Grey Fox, 1965.

Suknaski, Andrew. *Silk Trail*. Toronto: Nightwood Editions, 1985.

Wah, Fred. *Alley Alley Home Free*. Red Deer, AB: Red Deer College Press, 1992.

————. *Lardeau*. Toronto: Island Press, 1965.

————. "Margins into Lines: A Relationship." *Tish* 1–19. Ed. Frank Davey. Vancouver: Talonbooks, 1975. 82–83.

————. *Music at the Heart of Thinking*. Red Deer, AB: Red Deer College Press, 1987.

————. Open letter to Louis Zukofsky and rev. of *Blue Grass* 3 that features a selection of poems by Zukofsky titled "Found Objects 1962–1926." *Sum: A Newsletter of Current Workings* 3 (1964): 24–25.

————. *Pictograms from the Interior of B.C.* Vancouver, BC: Talonbooks, 1975.

———. "Propped Form—Ashes of Content." Transparency Machine Event 28. University of Windsor, ON, 2007. 1 February 2008, http://web4.uwindsor.ca/english. English; Podcasts and videos.

———. *So Far*. Vancouver, BC: Talonbooks, 1991.

———. *Waiting for Saskatchewan*. Winnipeg: Turnstone Press, 1985.

Williams, William Carlos. *The Collected Poems of William Carlos Williams*, Vol. I, 1909–1939. Ed. Christopher MacGowan. New York: New Directions, 1986.

———. *The Collected Poems of William Carlos Williams*, Vol. II, 1939–1962. Ed. Christopher MacGowan. New York: New Directions, 1991.

Zukofsky, Louis. *Louis Zukofsky: Selected Poems*. Ed. Charles Bernstein. New York: Library of America, 2006.

A Fred Wah Bibliography

Lardeau. Toronto: Island Press, 1965.

Mountain. Buffalo, NY: Audit Press, 1967.

Among. Toronto: Coach House Press, 1972.

Tree. Vancouver: Vancouver Community Press, 1972.

Earth. Canton, NY: Institute of Further Studies, 1974.

Pictograms from the Interior of B.C. Vancouver: Talonbooks, 1975.

Loki Is Buried at Smoky Creek: Selected Poetry. Vancouver: Talonbooks, 1980.

Owners Manual. Lantzville, BC: Island Writing Series, 1981.

Breathin' My Name with a Sigh. Vancouver: Talonbooks, 1981.

Waiting for Saskatchewan. Winnipeg: Turnstone Press, 1985.

Rooftops. Nobleboro, ME: Blackberry Books, 1987/Red Deer, AB: Red Deer College Press, 1988.

Music at the Heart of Thinking. Red Deer, AB: Red Deer College Press, 1987.

Limestone Lakes Utaniki. Red Deer, AB: Red Deer College Press, 1989.

So Far. Vancouver: Talonbooks, 1991.

Alley Alley Home Free. Red Deer, AB: Red Deer College Press, 1992.

Faking It: Poetics and Hybridity, Critical Writing 1984–1999. Edmonton: NeWest, 2000.

Isadora Blue. Victoria, BC: La Mano Izquierda Impresora, 2005.

Diamond Grill. Edmonton: NeWest Press, 1996, 2006.

Articulations. Vancouver: Nomados Literary Publishers, 2007.

Sentenced to Light. Vancouver: Talonbooks, 2008.

is a door. Vancouver: Talonbooks, 2009.

Mountain that has come over me in my youth
                green grey orange of colored dreams
        darkest hours of no distance
                        Mountain full of creeks ravines of rock
    and pasture meadow snow white ridges humps of granite
                ice springs trails twigs stumps sticks leaves moss
            shit of bear deer balls rabbit shit
        shifts and cracks of glaciation mineral
O Mountain that has hung over me in these years of fiery desire
    burns on your sides your many crotches rocked
                and treed in silence from the winds
    Mountain many voices nameless curves and pocked in shadows
                        not wild but smooth
        your instant flats flat walls of rock
                your troughs of shale and bits
    soft summer glacier snow
                    the melting edge of rounded stone
        and cutting of your height the clouds
            a jagged blue
                            your nights your nights alone
        your winds your winds your grass
                your lying slopes your holes your traps
        quick blurs of all my dreams
Mountain poem of life
    true and real
            reeling Mountain burning mind
    stand word stand letter
                voice in whisper secret repeating cries
        stand in rock stretch out
            in all ways to the timber line
    spread over all valleys run cool the waters down
            from luminous white snows
                your cracks

O creek song flow always an utter pure of coolness
spring from the rocks
sing in the hot thirst my sticky tongue
my jaw catch below the bridge
Yes my jaw for your waters hangs
catch of water soothe the sweat
sweet cold on teeth in flow and eddy
in swirl my gut it fills and bloats with fluid Mountain

even the eyes
    along the road the map plots
        move as once moved
      time took from
             even the eyes switch
     turn with each bend
       bridge the creeks cut
even the eyes the fences make
     and lumber yards the sawdust fills
        even the eyes scan
along a lake the ditches' bottles weed and beaches' sand
      or gravelled air of gravel
even the dust the eyes recall what the map shows
     as trail flag stop railway
          trestle the creosote planks
  or powerline the cut is or clearing the legs' relief
     from elevation intervals ridge to ridge
        the contour eyes make boundaries shot
   chains traverse the timber lease
       or lookout eyes look lookout of
even the eyes a lake is or creek fills
     and the map the eye is a circle makes
            the Mountain isn't

akokli (goat) creek

More music
in its name
than "goat"

Akokli rise
as the June
snow melts.

The forest
is dark above
the road above

the creek
the mountain
moves down

the jeep
moves down
the trees

the dark is
down among

the bumpy swells
of Akokli Creek.

Gold Hill

We stood there in Gold Hill's forest
    looking
at all that surrounded us
    that rock
this rock here this one
    was it here
he stopped by stooped down aside of
    and grabbed from the rock
    a piece of moss to wipe himself with
    said shIT!
this granite boulder's gold
    worth about
as he was an assayer also
    $70,000
but unable to move such a large rock himself
    chipped some proof
then went away to find help
    file the claim
but never found it after that day
    so
we stood there in Gold Hill's forest
    looking.

Among

The delight of making inner
an outer world for me
is when I tree myself
and my slight voice screams glee to him
now preparing his craft for the Bifrost
Kerykeion he said, the shore
now a cold March mist moves
down through the cow pasture
out of the trees
among, among

Poem for Turning

Move down
zigzag through
switchback
through sideways
move down there
move side right
move left
keep right angles
head front-wise
cleft earth hold
the fall-line
fall to trees
keep incline
be degrees
go corner
move side move
jut out

in boots road pick-up sidewise wide
three ruts
wheel ridge grass switch eyes move in
boots

in
heel
knee
cut side-hill
ditch run-off
move down
ricochet track
 line shove
spin out fall
back fall side
saw the forest

clear the creek
rock
split the sky
open roll dig
cover burn
 fill the fill
and cross the
bridge turn up
turn into turn
at it

For the Western Gate

Its hard to believe
Enough of this to make
The horizontal land appear
A place or highway
Here or in the starry sky
And trust my eyes to speak.

The sky was there last night
There above the dark range
Clear   over the mist and trees
That star, she said, is that
The look it sees us through?

Hard enough to see
One small point or passage
And take that the Gate
The by-way and a pass-word
Now to know I go as I look
Not otherwise   only
Through the mouth of eyes
I speak for myself I
Want to go out there   out
Over the view to look for

Havoc Nation

How the earth
dangles
eyeing over the geographical heap
now the nation smothers
lays onto the private magic state
its own fake imagination.
                               Backoff
into my own feet
and onto my own weight
leap and into her hair
Love tangles, in her eyes
Havoc sleeps.
                    "Cry Havoc"
and slip out the dogs of war.
The first woman will always be
the first woman and that
is a revelation.
                         How do you tell
someone elsewhere you live? Can you
reveal it as real a place
as they sometimes think you are?
                               In the mountains near here
there is a woman who is also crow.
She is overjoyed with tears
when she meets another likewise crow.
Even if you knew this
could you look her up?
                         I also know a man who is a tree
and he received a letter
from a friend back east which ends
"It must be a very real world where you are.
                                        Love, George"

That man is me
as well a revelation.

Well dangle then
the revelation
revolution nation
let slip the dogs of war
out your back door
Trees and Crows
are the ones what knows
this Havoc old Hav Ok
will stuff it in your Cry
this magic leaping tree
wiII never be the apple
of anyone else's Eye.

Hamill's Last Stand
for Gladys McLeod

1.

Our concern is tree-murder, harvest
of the forest (she's worried
they call it "timber") timber sale A04292
      structure wood
could be a rough political situation,
                      could be
we speak as trees, innocent understanding of ourselves
as things or places too, maybe farming
      but for the mess
left on the smouldering hillsides
                   and silting the creeks
maybe a new crop another lifetime, no care
for the names Hemlock, Balsam, Spruce
undone words from our own mouths,
                   no flowers anymore but
cubic feet seven million two hundred
                  and thirty-eight
thousand Cedar, Larch, White Bark Pine,
                trunk roots and
limbs scrapped trash-wood fuel
          for the bush-fires dirty
orange summer skyline, Lodgepole,
          White Pine, Other
Species, in other words
        strip it, all the growth
        for structure wood

core of our eyes to see and say it,
                              won't be taken
care of, hearts lost in the language
                       of public auction
only "profit" in the names, no talk
                  left about it, so set now
there is no argument, choices gone,
                            nothing left to say
Forest Ranger.

2.

house of structure wood all leaky
roof this morning in the rain

sits in the chimney flashing seeps
through to the roof joists and drips

still upright tree wood (branches?)
from the floor sill to cross-beams

what cells left without the bark, root-
less timbers stand in the doorways

and window frames its ok the house
is "appropriate," our real needs

do not profit us, the hillside trees
also leak the rain down to their roots.

3.

I admit the industry of it, hot
summer work, sweat and mosquitoes
in the headband of the hardhat, chain-oil,
whine of the diesel among the spruce
ehrrrrehrrr of the saw
to the heart-wood, I admit
the hi-baller works for a new pickup
each year, weekends in town
I admit his skill, I admit that he makes
a life of his own from it, with a grip
on the throttle lever, admit it

4.

Probably the trees are warming in the sun
the mud dries up and hardens on the roads
streams are full and muddy now in runoff
a whole forest stretches out the new rings
probably it all just stands there, amazed
with the steam rising up from clay banks
gravel shoulders glisten
     in the morning light
bridge planks shed roofs ditches a contour
part of a scene, probable and amazing
for the sun, warmer now towards the end
of March, a forest moves towards the light.

Chain

1.

The idea of it. Pictures form and the topography
gets carried around in a head. Sometimes the feet
find out what a trick the mind is. A necessary
disguise for what the heart expects. But the Abney
Rule and Compass are equally off. And so we move
in on the new territory only to trip and fall over our
imaginations, get lost.

2.

Snowed a few inches last night. Went up to the
Giant's Kneecap – freezing wind snow and whiteout
at the top. Skied down into Joker Creek a ways before
we realized we were in the wrong valley.

3.

There are times moving through the bush so fast
I fade into everything around me. Zigzag, switchback
and sidehill force a fadeout between body and earth.
Such a dance. Touch is some thing itself. A flash.

4.

Everything's out there larger elsewhere and then
I add myself who's watching.

5.

Via the car journeying over the surface is when its
flat. Maybe boats on still water too or skiing
across the frozen lake. By plane its always there
and back so more a line.

6.
Look out of the cave-mouth at an arched horizon,
cut-off sky and alabaster rock wall limits. We
see a night sky, the arch of stars, some heaven.

7.
The size of a river = its original ridges.

8.
We moved over the tables making our various tests
for identification – hardness, specific gravity,
streak, etc. Just as though we were about to cook
and eat it all talk shifts to a rumour of serpentine
on True Blood Mountain.

9.
Lyles Adopola. Sweet smelling orange mint.

10.
The Xthonic inhabitants of the sea, ridge-dwellers,
known as 'the steady ones'.

11.
One can imagine how difficult it might be to navigate
a course through some creeks, trails, and ravines
which are measured both in terms of a surface (the
map) and the underside of someone's idea of the
place (the story).

12.
The magical alchemical inversion of it is that it
is already.

13.
Duncan M. says he dearly loves his own back yard.
Now I do too. The only test we have for it is
the unavoidable picture.

14.
High in the mountains, high on a mountain, and spin.
To ride this horizon of a thousand peaks and sky
makes me dig my heels into the scree and ice and
lean back hard, just to hold on even.

15.
Silence leads – sinking into the viscera – gently –
head feels lighter and drained – a thin, fragile
wire open now – mind of all the air surrounds me –
arms and shoulders fall relaxed – carefully and
softly my body is lifted back up refreshed and
presented to the food – mouth holds to the first
taste which fills my head stretched out now over
the lake and the day.

16.
I get scared sometimes when I'm alone in the bush,
especially at dusk when the stumps and rocks become
grizzly bears. Never handled that aloneness, passage
to becoming all one over extended time in unknown
strange surroundings except to squint, peer, grope
and fumble.

17.

I was sick, very sick. And I hoped for deep sleep.
It seemed to me that the bed was in an east-west
axis and should be lying north-south. But true or
magnetic north I did not know. A cow elk appeared
to me, in a valley, so I checked my compass and
headed north.

severance spring water
wasp or hornet who cares
it was a toxic arrow full of information of Another World a stream of itself
immense ejaculation knockout zapping nerve box
synapse blackout another place so beautiful Pauline that's where I am
Pauline
No   No   Here uh   yes Here I   uh
slapped me back to bathroom pain and muscle struggle I was gone there
taken over
some chemical creek flowed through the dream in darkness
there was nothing to look at or any others taking part
she slapped and yelled at me
I didn't want to return
it was so beautiful this textured cool caress
the spring water I splashed on my eye
Sunday morning
Sun Trees
A Loss   A Dream
Voices in the rooms outside me
He needs
adrenalin stretched out and holding on
Needles   Shapes   Stomach (the vulnerable
fix the spring get the tools
barbed wire
his foot at the nest
bango
a distance   road   cold   fear   dead weight
jaw
the viscous fluid flowing through all my body helpless now
that power the wasp informs me of
given
such a look
at the grid of action the bloodstream's also part
the sting
it signaled it was ready for and took
on the way to the hospital she said
just keep breathing I hadn't even considered it.

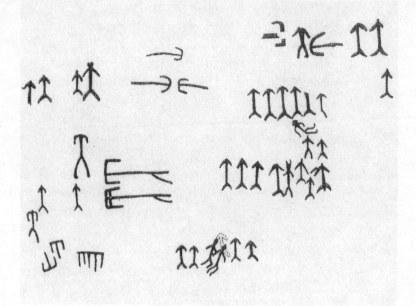

September spawn
fish weirs everywhere
all through the narrows.

Upstream, upstream.

A feast for all of us
cousins and old friends
everybody dancing
like crazy, eh?

        nv s ble
tr ck

We are different
from one another
in the space between us
a lot happens
more than of only you or I

the air
or through it all
(dog, turtle, beaver
fallen trees by the roadside
I remember)
I have come to be
no different from them

one by one one can
become the other

such as night serves t
o show day's stars

sounds of o and ree
tryi-, try to make breath
sounds that make (sky)
mine (me) to breath

                (see breath
                        out in front of myself
                        as a white mist in the winter air

or some school teacher read us a story
about the arctic and how cold cold is
so cold someone's words had been frozen in the air
and years later when it warmed up
language popped out right in front of them
right out of the air
breath
which makes sound from my body
air which flys out of me
through o and ree
oooooory   ooooory
breaking open as spittle would crackle in the frozen air

              crystal

Breathe dust like you breathe wind so strong in your face little
grains of dirt which pock around the cheeks peddling against
a dust-storm coming down a street to the edge of town in
Swift Current Saskatchewan or the air walked out into the
fields across from Granny Erickson's house with a few pails
of water to catch gophers over by the glue factory downwind of
all the horses corralled their shit and hay smell whipped over
the grass and the smell of prairie water as unmoved water doesn't
move is stale or even rancid but the air along the prairie road
by Uncle Corny's farm first thing on a clear summer sunday
morning and in winter how the snow smelled like coal when
I maybe later in Trail B.C. up the alley behind our place
my mother needed water to melt on top of the wood cook stove
so she sent me out with my sleigh and a galvanized washtub
to collect the snow so dirty in the city I scraped off the top
few inches before I put my shovel in and then packed it into the
tub and back to the house and stove air hot and steamy pink over
the stove my mother what did she need that water for I don't know
but where somewhere the snow smelled like coal or is it back in
Swift Current and cold so cold it smelled of cold I don't remember
maybe we had oil there we did later in Nelson and I had to go
out into the shed and pump a bucket of oil from a 45-gallon
drum for the stove in the living room but the shed had a coal
bin too coal for the stove in the kitchen at night coal dust
even later filling up Pearson's furnace hopper every three
days move it shovel full across the basement the dust even
later in the summer play anywhere someone's coal bin settled
into my nose and the oilyness of it on the skin I rode down the
hill outside the house on Victoria on a coal shovel I hit a
rock and had the wind knocked out of me I was dying and couldn't
even tell anyone as they walked by but stood and waved my arms
and flailed the message without air

Sigh. A tenuous slight stream of air escapes through a high
point midway up the chest. At night, during sleep, this light
puff of breath is part of running and falling.

Night and breath, the moonlight, him breathing hard as he walks
along the black road on a cold November night, the stars wear
thin. At least he's thinking that and then he says to himself
"the trees" and "they are there as they have always been in the
dream or in the memory of them." So the cold air condenses on
his mustache and he blows out a puff of air which then glistens
out in the moonlight as jewels in front of himself.

Home before you know it. The stove still warm. He talks to
himself because thinking has become words in his mouth and the
pictures from the day coalesce with the pictures of the night so
that he talks in his sleep (he thinks). The language comes into
the room with him and touches the sides of the stove, turns out
the dining room light, undresses.

Then the thin stream of air from his nostrils heads for his toes
but before it gets there, before it settles into his bones,
before it spreads out into the night, it sets out over a world.

A hight
e at beneath
the heaven
she heavy
over ethe
every as in
ide David

Aug 5

*We tour Hong Kong today in a bus with a guide hyping
photos of ourselves. I start taking notes re places I've seen
my father since he died. I think of him here in this city, in
transit, 60 years ago. See first statues and full of colour
(white is death, why Ethel didn't want a white coffin for
him, red for marriage) numbers too, 9 for longevity and
active life, 8 for wealth (there it is the 8-spot lottery
Grampa's gambling smile confirmed).*

Numbers in everything said
    clatter each block commerce tooled
fronted with "making" some piece or all of it
    "lucre" personal contrivance shuttle
family woven decades ahead first
    his father and even him and his son
place attribute magnetic magic
    like that tailored jade street single
attempt to move made so that "generation" gets
    skyline to 1997 after direct incant from
latitude Cantonese genocide nil hope stalled not
    to edit out immigrant identity cancel
head count not really meaningful money exchange
    added up with calculation mind counts the years
abacus clicks in the market stall can't wait
    for seasonal switch typhoon number late
afternoon maybe a winter somewhere in his mind
    but far away, far away.

Music at the Heart of Thinking 1

Don't think thinking without heart no such
separation within the acting body takes a step
without all of it the self propelled into doing the
thing (say, for example, the horse) and on the
earth as well picking up the whole circuit feet
first feel the waves tidal and even outside to
moon and sun it's okay to notate only one of
those things without knowing fixed anyway
some heart sits in the arms of

Music at the Heart of Thinking 6

Sentence the true morphology or shape of the
mind including a complete thought forever
little ridges little rhythms scoping out the total
picture as a kind of automatic designing device
or checklist anyone I've found in true thought
goes for all solution to the end concatenates
every component within the lines within the
picture as a cry to represent going to it with the
definite fascination of a game where the number
of possibilities increases progressively with each
additional bump Plato thought

Music at the Heart of Thinking 28

Salt for the tongue's Heart heartening desire
paradoxical cold and hot Canadian presence/
absence mime's right action right mind et al
simple terms a vision Avison teaches frames
leaks hollows and flows in '63 she and Olson
walked out to the cliffs at Point Grey
oceanward falling west to "placeless place" he
says she did not walk out if you see his West 6
but I remember the day and it wasn't evening it
was afternoon he says for him the most impor-
tant conversation and event was this Pacific
continental wedge "that marge of the few feet
make the difference between the West, and the
Future" magnet in the word finds this salt
exciting if there was no wall there wouldn't be
the heat not just "Is" and "is not" come clear as
she says but how much "in the tongue's
prison" of the dream this overlaps "the rest is
history."

Music at the Heart of Thinking 50

Going through the language of time.
Chronometrics. Horologicals. A book of years.

I like the water in it. And the footprints.
That movement. As you look for words
"sans intermission."

Of course it's the heart. Pictograph –
                                    pictogram.
Epigram – epigraph. Cardiogram. Histograph.
The paw again.

Cellular. Un instant. Je vais voir si je la trouve
dans ce livre.
It's that "yelping pack of possibilities"
the hour as the order.

The predication, the pre-form of foot
in snow, log
on truck, finding out it never was lost,
                                    fooling.

Music at the Heart of Thinking 55

Map of streets stream of dreams
map of creeks street of cream, fragments
and imago imprint, geomance a glyph,
a place on earth, under, or from it.

Name's broken letters maybe
words your body made.
Idiot bridges to parts of our selfs still lost
in the palindrome.

A found chain on the coffeetable,
Some Scapes as a bookmark
to automobile between 3 and 6;
flex, flux, flooding, fl–

   (ə Creekscape: Looking Upstream)

Fred Was. Fred War. Fred Wan. Fred Way.
Fred Wash. Fred Wag. Fred Roy. Fred What.

Creek water hits rock with hollow sound.

Music at the Heart of Thinking 77

Earth seems comfortably familiar and sometimes
strangely familial so deja vu green but when it becomes
unfamiliar or downtown centre decentral displaced place
of all things negative capability a positive incapacity to
not know knowing narrates not just Wordsworth's big
something else that is determines the rainbow of silence
and noise with a clear distortion at the edges of the
supratactic acoustics at one end and cosmology at the
other underneath dichten condensare's ambiguous ochre
dysfunction fragmented rotten Rockies decidedly what's
called fear of the hatchtop or self-departure mountain
arrived and derived alter-native this making strange still
oddly tied to wobbling terra firma no matter what.

Music at the Heart of Thinking 78

Music here like the foot and door quick check of the
imprint assuring story construction and that
unquestioning privilege of narrative as knowing the only
fiction seeming to be the reader everything else counted
for or lost only momentarily in the cacophony of
murmured concern that is itself distorted by a
comfortable pre-text almost uncannily like the Spaniard's
view of the new world old habits and all so scenario is
not so much a truth like metaphor but only the afterbirth
what happens later serves to trample the building debris
after treading the winepress alone entwined by the
promise of riddles and certain chronicles just for fun
since the novel is supposedly only a space project time'll
have to launch the rockets of textuary running the line so
that a useful physics gets applied to the physiology here
literally heat and its measurement but I don't mean the
body's natural energeic plot but more a form of ritual or
what becomes speech loaded and violent corresponding
to such sad things as Virgil's wolf in the fold and the
anger of Amarylis nothing of which counts in the
predicates of the ontology of anger even this irritating
gabble at the edge of the page book takes over from the
horizon not as a refusal of silence indeed but then not to
neglect the echo either have you ever seen a space not
occupied by some sort of grammar the point here to
hyphen promise so that you recognize other events as
more immediate targets but that's prose for you always
hanging around to identify the self what a Quebec poet
calls these eternal calculations. that's what I want also the
page running and stars of intonation like swimming
along the ladder since anger has this prototype that
includes retribution I'd suggest canceling the order and
simply leaving the discontinuous as mothers and fathers

period being written like that isn't so bad but even so imagine the possibility of literal language-life a kind of narrative civilization that could tatoo for itself itself and read only the past tense because in fact that's the only hay to cut unless you'd rather consider picturing someone else's lost garden I must admit I've thought of everything as edible vibration for the pharynx and that's one of those things you've got to judge prior to recollection if the essential tools are borrowed off the bench how can we mend our own soul or is this only frivolous ongoing law as unself-conscious of denouement as poor assaulted reader of this facade used here simply to return you to a resonance of recognition much like a boring Ontario horizon replaces your attention with notions of elsewhere but what are you going to do is fact fiction or are they both strangers to music which is as much space as time by the way sound articulates distances and fields and not only pace to verify the solo variant of course to mobilize subject do we need story but not as the cruelty of logic and the ultimate "game" only to tell trace and the range of passions that cause that inmost core to reverberate actually shake the model up and kick past the door if we are right our map has considerable light for the labyrinth my daughters are the kind of immediate people I'm thinking of who would never scoff a feast or possibly the goal isn't worth it diction moments usually bring new weather and all of us possess a lot of randomness so why not confront this stuttering then let the floods flash but first find out if we're on to gesture and try not to let it signify ceremony but housework that hum to the inner ear fragmented into short songs of plotless therefore dreary life imitating a wandering or dreaming mind whatever the mode ex out those long moments from the future as if we knew why we choose any route but the one home except to think we are already there the slowest being the quickest though sometimes someone comes in with news of the others this emotional torture gets to be a bit vast if you let it take over as a mass synapse a little growing awareness of stride will get the smack in the door out.

Music at the Heart of Thinking 89

I've always had trouble with the ingenious engine as a suffix of graded wanting love or prayer especially kindergarten stifled kid as a kind of person who might extend racism or even keep me off the block your kindred jammed the oceans cognitive shot freeborn got then similar to most of the inborn tutelary spirits everywhere naive seed of Enyallion or old chip off the old rock and that's congenital heart buds gyna gendered and warped up tighter than a Persian rug how ginger's almost nicer than being born but that's just taste.

Music at the Heart of Thinking 93

Any gravel road's ok by me or is that an ordering
intervention so long as it's not pure highway to the end
of the void without my story our narrative's just a bunch
of rotten windfalls under the apple tree of someone else's
eye a statistical cluster made up to cover up and that
stupid notion of a project as sticking it to everyone else
instead of girdling yourself to the entelecheic text
underfoot that dreamt you long ago

an earth doesn't add up to the only implicate map
ethnos is and

the new doesn't have to be the purety nation is at
least some Love pictographed without lexicon gets us to
the grannies grammar

Music at the Heart of Thinking 98
(PEARAGRAPHS for Roy Kiyooka)

A collection of pomace. Left over. Residue. Pome poem. Fruit, of looming back yard pear tree. Windowed lost love, seasoned symmetry of gaze. Words to hang onto, picked, plucked, pared, preserved. Or rain/frost-rotted brown on top of the camper.

Nest. Branch and sky for hair. Dream space where the eye-shaktra's rooted up prime before the mind's eye in growth rings fluttered flowered house of interlimb, mesh of mindingness, net work, nest work.

Some bright beam lights up behind the eyes, or through the greenery, truths of all sorts writing pang and time. Tall is as old is. That's a fact. Things to put a bite on, the bark. Getting to the char-core heart with word-worm tunneling. Put an ear to.

Low roar of shakuhachi waves. Enki drumming on the cedar. Hammered words said beep bent forgotten all but the ever-resonating thud even the paper-clean dry seed-head split and distant sound of frost released from brittle memory pod.

Old dogs of war words let loose as forkt birds slipping the private magic state into talking tree. Listen. Love words. Language paired and othered over the geographical heap, dangled from a canopy called earth-as-sky. Caw. Coo.

Facing the old yin-yang turbine round the night sky weaving its stars into the tree tops shade upon shadow questioning distance upon distant sites sign voice weather noting exed ever only spins plus minus minus minima plus.

After the throttle cutting of white inked into body along with the sigh of staining the world with the same body. What a river such tangible surfaces usher singing; its banks cut too with smells and other signs of shape or touch tuned with Meloids.

Word as seed preserve brings up the notion of rotten language composting for the progeneration of itself and the ripe vocable as soft and juicy palpable but for the bite of belief and the Bering Isthmus migration so far from the Cantonese pollen.

Chinatown walking through the food smelling and then sitting down in a booth to taste the birds-nest soup or any noodle late night neon ragtime all alone in the dawn music Virgil's vigil down the street and home again home again.

Stirred-up word leaves equal to birds' startled whoosh and the morphophonic fruiting of the great vowel shift(s) syllable canting the old prayer wheel so familiar as the resonating fat of the adjective, you know, like "Summertime".

The tropisim of allowing the range of stimulation (in this case, sky) and avoiding such an indicator as clarity of outline (that is, fingering it) puts the poet's nose to the wind so that bite has surface (in fall, that could mean frost).

Yes, there are a few of those brushes with sudden silence. The "great" hush. A slight stunning of the uttering tongue diverts to rainforest and you know OM is AM somewhere on the hermes dial. Even the trees wait, rooted.

Here the wickerwork of wonder prevails, especially seasonally, especially winter. Night turns too. That's when the griddle glows with answers, that's when the porch of stars or clouds twigs to the forecast, that's when the eyes get used to the dark.

This stoniness that comes to life, unfetters itself from heap by song and the crazy clicking of the compass needle from side to side, something ringing ahead, something diamond, vertebraeic, maybe something bonelike in the name.

Sometimes it's just word as a reflective buoy nunning and canning entrance to the (h)arbour. At others, smell's left to gauge place, expecially in the morning. The ode as a jar for dead fingernails. Pears, breathing through their skin.

Here's the tree traveller with news from the roots. For the poet that's the "heavenly" one, the one growing down from above. Not just dream. The tune is reflective: the image of the tree shows a tree. Such is home and the authority of love.

The tree-talk hears preaction (ie, just thinking about it) as a plot to rejuvenate the locomotor birth-breath effect (you know, when the sap rises) because there always seems to be an un-or de-chat to simulate houseness.

Layered into west-coast leafery is another homing device between the legs for birds, rivers, salmon, spawning gravel, and smouldering midden heaps. All old time warm, damp copulas charting ocean's peaks to get some home again.

Mother tongue tied lost ungendered gendering potent cone-seed to burst birth in any chance fire only words green branching into childhood pink Eve's apple stuck in man's throat all forest foreign but for the pear tree.

Behind this tree-braille on the slivered moon-pear of a page is his "screech" and behind that some solitary hollering of the pome poem as proper, as in *proprio*, vessel for any world-preserved jar of memory keeps listening for.

Tell-tale leaf-light filtered photosynthetic compost haunted by the house syntax. Paper page so under the thinking thumb, but then the word baggage tsunamis forth and tosses, say, the persona of language's song which then just dangles and spins.

Ancientness moving in on the dream of falling. Air drama, into the earth. Leaf-word-paper-skin-mold, moist churnowing of a tongue once flowered container of the "well" sprung within body sapling dappled skylight seeded.

ArtKnot 1

Take anything Max Ernst you fish as much as
the birds eyes horses so the eyes are the same the
eyes are not always the same look right into the
wood like heart right? say through plaster-cast
dactyllic to feel in a knot eyes and in the wood eyes
out of the wood or a figure cut from Un Chinois
Egare A Lost (Bewildered) Chinaman he called it
natural history you can imagine the silk print since
youth stare at things at any things.

ArtKnot 2

encaustic "you"
literal vertical history
making french factory garments
your painting called "Slate"
imagine time made up
of materials besides "wood, various
papers, pins, powder
pigment, felt
pen, graphite,
india ink, mask-
ing tape,
plexiglass"

I believe you

but to not know thinking
whatever you called it
is never impossible so
the contemporary past "information"
so necessary to use stuff and other
wonder about it then
never name it, Irene

ArtKnot 4

the Idea, Henri
moves

"Mouvements 1950" in sumi sign
tachism repeats

seeing
saying

appearances and agitations
not just the rock surfaces
mind, too, splashes
expression all over

that mescal uneasiness
quivers

why you studied medicine
yet became a sailor
suddenly 1922 "art"
and February '83
into the Seibu in lkebukuro

they know, they know
you have a hint of something
dirt
at the surface you thought
to whisper
a little gossip

Hermes Poems

For all that place
hidden behind glass
and silent tortoise-stone shell
rocks for eyes

further
walked footsore for years
just to have a look
snuck up on smouldered night
seen cloaked by day

The harbour's for the ear and the view. Out there a minor fourth
fog horn claims large chunks of life. Sun glints off a powerboat
windshield. Someone waves between waves, disapears. Boats bob.
Risky staring

Victory Square
lots of chairs
for sitting on
outside in

Sillowing of work buzz at the edges, kitchen shadows. Sudden departure.
Pecky meandering. Drumming day.

Hermes is a package of crackers

in Ierapatra
a motor bike
a taxi stand
a tour agency
rentacar

broken windmill spokes
solar water heater
man on a donkey

a blue plastic bag
a red plastic bag
a hotel in Rhodos

turkish

Hermes is a snack bar
at the corner of Georgiou Kyrmixali
and Nikolaou Plastira
smoking

a hotel near the Plaka

and he comes from the mouth of an animal
on top of a cement mixer called Heracles

There's a goose sitting on a nest on top of a piling. What at first I thought
was her mate isn't. Turns out to be a loon, further out, bobs, then looks,
pokes its nose into the lake, under. Looks down from that noonday
above. Poke, poke. Beyond all this creative stuff are the mountains. A
trail turns around a large boulder. Subito.

Hrbr

water
scooters
boats fish

eat out
at night
and a light

                    house har-
                    bour kalimera
                    ave maria

                    hawa
                    evening
                    our mothers too

                    havoc

Men's mothers and the doorway bavardage. Arms folded, hips to post,
toe tapping. This is the shore, the ebb in ebony.

                    Cretan wheels scribble
                    push at the walls of the island
                    night after long night

Translate coop and the desire for a perfect fit. Kaboom. Snap a vector
until some word for steering gets there. Gyproc or wood.

                    "if one falls and..."

jet-skyed
sand-filled
star-specked
girl-drenched
steel-netted
feet-pressed
house-whited
mortar-channeled
sun-paired
sandal-quiet
wrist-brushed
heart-weighted
"rock-hung
chain...
broken"

Not this is what you see but this is what you say. You seeing. This trip a kind of samskara to scare out the europe ghosts. It's as close as you've come to the old, old world — dead, dead europe. But you say it simplex, just to yourself. That's no good for these similes, one, then many. The world needs to be talked to, sung to. Some blind thing or poet. Some word rivering alongside.

The Poem Called Syntax

We live on the edge of a lake called Echo.
I love this notion that noise makes itself,
so the lake holds all noise in its depths
and when the dog barks it gets it from the lake.

About nine thousand feet above these lakes (all lakes)
there is a geometry of sound, something like Plato's cave of noise.
It is from that construct the dog's bark takes shape,
a resounding of an earlier bark conditioned by the alpine.

History and physics. Acoustic paradigms in a bog of algae.
When I tell all my cousins and friends about this
they'll come to live on the shores of this lake and clean it up.
From the balconies of their summer homes they'll ask a lot of questions.

Dead in My Tracks: Wildcat Creek Utaniki

Saturday, July 29/89
Oh golden, Golden morning!

West of Golden we leave the trans-Canada and drive north about 60 k up Blaeberry River past Doubt Hill. From the chopper site we can see south to Howes Pass , a long sweep of valley brilliant in a pillowed mid-summer heat-haze. An hour's spent wrapping the cars and trucks in chicken wire (old paranoid alpine parking-lot visions of the imaginary porker chewing our tires and rad hoses). Camp's just west, a ten-minute bezier curve, swirl, and plop up Wildcat Creek, on a west slope facing east to the contintental divide ridgeline of the B.C./Alberta boundary.

Ringed by glaciers as usual

Ayesha, Baker, Parapet.

While we set up camp during the afternoon I'm in a global mode, you know, the simultaneity of the world going on right now. Paris. Kyoto. Beijing. The pavement of Tiananmen Square, the hotlines sniffing out the dissidents, CBC bulletin even e-mail media drama of the last two months still in the air, even up here, radioless, only antennaed in my bones (our name is bones, and your name is my name).

My Borders are Altitude

and silent

<pre>
                    a pawprint's cosine
      climate   from the lake to the treeline
               all crumbly under foot at the edges
                cruddy summer snow melt
        soft wet twig and bough-sprung alpine fir
                                    but more than this
        height
           is my pepper
</pre>

(China

    don't)

    Now

(broken breaths contour intervals at the next 100 feet and then the sky-remembered night on the plateau above the Saskatchewan Qu'appele oh stars what solitude your blue line and flight or weight the inverse holds me shoulder-to-shoulder my clouds as alpine meadows Newton would have cut yet minds find bandwidth in this topos-parabola chaos around the earth house

    Here's this

        stone under heathered turf

    back bent as I dig and ruffle   sacrum

        drawn to the music

                a slow and daily pelvic tilt of elevation

is this numbered boundary nowhere, I'm

close to 7000 here, maybe I'll just do the horse

        not to hold the world

                just touch, complete

        the circuit

        borders such thin thoughts (apples of our eyes)

                selvage yesterday's Tiananmen

        a power-line buzz above, along my spine, my legs

go up and down

        heart all summer-heavy

        with the people

Sunday, July 30

We hike east across the valley toward Mistaya Mountain, as far as a scree slope on the south side of a grano-diorite carbuncle so massive we're left only to pick and chip below the heel of.

Each rock vectors through the eyes to the height of the stomach and stops me, dazzles, dead in my tracks. Such singular surfaces are impossible to avoid. Eyes tumble click, stop and stare, stop, stare at pink molten sunset rivers of limestone, sawtooth schist embedded. But at this rate the hike's all history, pleistocene.

No animals, no print, no scat. (Goat tracks? Too faint now to be sure.)
No sky-mirrored glacial swimming holes today.
No fresh water. Heather very dry. The bees buzz. Butterflies.
Doze in the sun at the bottom of a scree slope waiting for the others.

> *sugar* of their struggle death
> in China's humid night so far away
> maybe that's the simplest equation
> for the headwaters
> television's human river
> and now the sun decreases
> the friction. The fingers
> of my right hand trace
> a band of quartz. My eyes sink
> under the brim
> far away
> but not so far away.

Monday, the 31st
Today we climb the same side of the valley as yesterday. But now we've
taken a keep-more-to-the-left route to a neck or col between Alberta
and B.C., under Mistaya. Lunch beside a snowpatch lake.

> when deconstruing rock
> hold back the crude and the harsh
> or take "reality" for simple target
> the sun
>   a nation as large as China
> is just another scheme for thirst and war
> another centered project tunneling earth
>   (my father's fingers poked wet into the mud of
>   a rice paddy
> rumours, the same large-spun sky here
> in the thin air and during the long winter
> quartz grows with the sparkle of a bridge
> every stone on this mountain clicks
> some old biotic tumbler locked
> unlocked sadness

not of the hundred-blossomed mountain
not of the nine-millenia incense
but of the dragon-slit tongue silenced
youth before old age

After-lunch drowsiness sets in under the warmth of the sun; no birds sing; not so far away the glacier rivers roar in the July heat.

shale shard weep shard shale weep shale weep shard shale weep shale weep shard shard weep shale shard weep shale weep weep shhh

Those rocks this morning on the way up appeared full of signs and messages. So I walked around in a meander and kind of grilled each striated spot for information, news of the conglomerate earth.

or

ee

ent

The others' words around me buzz and fall like horseflies. Alberta looks busy from this side; Jasper/Banff another of those new equations to satisfy war's glacial thirst. Ice-blue sky-line jet-tracked.

ent

re. Pren

eur. Prende

The wooden handle of an ice axe stuck in the snow: "When making an ax handle," the pattern is occasionally too far off. Somewhere else. Out of sight, "man." Out of mind.

snow pond fed by two large drifts vectored off of morraine.
no real fish.
the Beijing hotline surfaces as jet track reminder
through the high blue air
then sinks at news of the killings.
deep, like a floating thermostat.
deep, like a disappearing hook.
baited.

Tuesday, August 1

I didn't sleep very well last night because I had to get up as breakfast helper this morning -fretted about the alarm on my wrist-watch being loud enough and so now mid-afternoon, sit on a slope above what the camp's come to call "crystal gardens" on the cool (windy) side of a grassy knoll tired and lulled by the rush of waterfall across the valley and above this alleyway that led us here full of crystals dangled and hidden for years we poke under little rock ledges.

Quiet here. Light breeze to keep the horseflies down. I glass across a valley to a slope, for yesterday's tracks, but they've melted out. Pan back to a blurry knoll of purple yellow red pink and white on green with songs (I Don't want a Sickle) I can't get out of my head and there're the others, after-lunch sprawl on the heather, Pauline reading in her flower book.

> smoke in the wind, the forest below
> porcupine under the wire quietly chewing our tires
> is that it
> smoke in the city,
>   slow sweep sweep of a broom in the square

Small thunderstorm coming around Trapper Peak should force us down the hill, while on this beared-over gopher-searching mountainside I linger, stopped, can't keep my eyes off the rocks and surfaces surging to not so much arrest myself in all this "otherness" as greedily scour the dripping quartz for crystal jewels for my daughters. Something lucky, something old. Something eight-spot rooted in rock, fatherness ancestral distance cut.

Hand-held Pictostone

from above Wildcat rockscape of old Renaissance bullet hole or navel with tracks going out the sides a type of Malthusian linear function along the aisles of a Saturday afternoon matinee forever pocked with edge and gouged embedded pebble from distant beach a cracked and weathered map of textured tilt propellor hummed out from omphalic sedimentary lint enough to tell story's history warped high enough in the diurnal headlines from Beijing and Shanghai so that a geologist imagining fake fish in a fake lake scrapes around the edges for shrapnel but me I think in my own mittened photos of the life look out of and far away from these threads through the hole to continue the prospect beyond impact of landing very hard and fast and past the anima button.

New moon tonight.

Wednesday

A wet day. Drizzle started last night after days of heat. The snow-line is about 8500 feet this morning. Very cool all day, off and on rain and sleet, some hail. And no respite tonight so now I sit/lie in our tent at 9 p.m. still light enough to write. I've put on my toque and gloves. No thought. Just body.

A few of us walked up the valley on the other side of Wildcat Creek and crossed many feeder creeks and the glacier river at the head of the valley. I had to take off my pants and boots once. The water came up to just above the knees. Memoried on and off all day crossing Toby morraine years ago with my brother and Loki and how that crossing, just below the crotch, rejuvenated bruised ligaments. This time my feet remain ice all day.

All these rocks. Constant mirror and prescence in my eyes. More rocks than grains of sand in the whole world, I bet someone. Intricate pattern, surface, keeps stopping boot in pitch for eye to zoom. Sometimes I stop and try translating the imago-grammatic surfaces. What do I look for? This I-Chinging the earth for some other Gate of Heavenly Peace, monotoned loudspeaker in the Square signaling "Go home and save your life," old, embedded said-again family bone-names?

Scale of shale
jamb stone, lintel, henge.

When the door's open
there's nothing to catch the eye.

Except the sun (blink). Now this tent
on the outside of a non-scaled phenomenon.

We'll see, Fred says to himself, the tree
as much a cinnabar flag as

— the mountains folded and folded.
"with uncountable broken arms and legs floating..."

This sky of clouds, new grass, melon
summer fields creased .

By forcing them into the centre of the square
the indelible occupies the heart until next time.

These "basins of attraction"
these grains, these fractal editions.

Night swoops very low
just a reminder.

Thursday, 8/3/89

This morning I sit in the tent writing and try to situate the play in this place. The world today feels all stage. Nothing moves. A set set. There are the huge mist hackles clinging to the mountains, but no history.

Far, far down the valley a chainsaw whines.
At night now some of the creeks disappear.
Winter.

Friday, August 4/89

This last day we hike up to the col between Peto and Mistaya but get caught in a cold mist/fog. Just behind the gauze the oval of the sun teases. The cover didn't break so we don't go further than the snow field. We spend the rest of the day circumnavigating the head of the valley and several glacial lips up and down and home and that's eight and a half hours to a spaghetti dinner and the sky lifting to a blue evening.

Now nearly 9 o'clock and the mosquitoes, after days of rain, are up for it.

Out of the corner of my eye more rocks. And out an ear I hear a few birds sing their particular song, not solitary: the creeks rush and gurgle down to the valley below. In a corner of my mind is tomorrow's two and half hour hike out to the trailhead and then the long drive home. But nowhere else.

<pre>
          clear stingin' peaks
                         rock green moss
                                       campion
               all surface news
                                 inked
          to the bloated stone heroes
                         massed alongside Mao's mausoleum
          same shards here
                              within the square
                                          a "percolation
                        network"
          five lines,
                     five soldiers a line
                                    duende stone
          thano-stone
</pre>

The Poetry of Fred Wah / 61

Hey, Man

Juan Jose he
is valid
he sings
all the way
to Vallodolid.
What's that he said

"polloco"?
Or did he say we saw
the zapalote.

Hey, Man!
he's a buzzard
with his bones
all over his shirt
on the way
to Chemax.

And he speaks fast
the real stuff.
Let's take a taxi
to Tixcacal Tuyub.

He says his uncles
are his mother's brothers
saying, singing
with that bottle in his hand
he's ringing.

Wind him up
with movies, books
handsome smile
in his white jipijapa.
Hey, Man!
he's the one
from Mazatlan.

(sentenced)

is not
the string
of words
a sentence

is not
the voice
comes out
another's

is not
the thought
complete
before it

speak
is not
the mind
a knotted

string not
words that
only seem
not meant

to mean
or sent
not strung
to end

but tied
to cradle
each
to each

Ripraps (Louis Cabri) and Afterwords (Fred Wah)

Riprap #1: Linguistics

Maybe not so much anymore, but linguistics has been, as you know, a very significant paradigm for poets and their readers, theorizing and historicizing both the world in the word and the word in the world. Linguistics informs my introduction to this selection of your poems. I believe that you studied linguistics in university. There's an engagement with linguistics in your writing, at many levels. Lexical signs: In "Music at the Heart of Thinking 6," the very first word is "sentences." "MHT 77" includes the phrase "supratactic acoustics." "MHT 93" has the chestnut "grannies grammar." There are many others. More broadly, in your Windsor talk ["Propped Form—Ashes of Content," 13 March 2007, in the Transparency Machine Series], you describe "paradigms of poetic form," a notion of paradigm that can be taken as drawn from linguistics.

> The rupture of the page around 1960 was phonetic. That is, the poem (and its music) could be lifted off of the page, out of the eyes, and into the ear. What had been silent (the cryptic "message" underneath the lines) was, attractively, suddenly (because of the Beat poets) possible as a language event (in real time).
>
> I was studying music composition at UBC in 1960 when I took Warren Tallman's poetry course to spend some time with my girlfriend Pauline Butling. His class introduced me to William Carlos Williams's interest in more natural North American language rhythms and I soon discovered that poetry composition, with its attention to phonetics and intonation patterns, could be as particular as music composition. Another crucial course at that time was an introductory linguistics course offered by Ron Baker; most of the *Tish* poets (Kearns, Bowering, Davey, etc.) took that course. That led me to do graduate work in linguistics and poetry, and in Buffalo I worked with Henry Lee Smith Jr. on approaches to prosodic analysis more suited to recent shifts in modernist poetry. I became intrigued by the distinguishing and differentiating features of phonology and morphology and ideas like Samuel Levin's "paradigmatic thought suffixes" (the conjunction of thought and rhyme, sound and meaning). The proximity of music to poetry, then, was an opening I couldn't resist.
>
> The *MHT* series has mostly used the prose poem and thus the sentence as a basic unit of composition. The weight of the sentence as

central engages a wide range of underlying morphological and syntactic thought, all of that discursive terminology I had learned from descriptive linguistics. "Music at the Heart of Thinking," with its run-on run-over sentences offered a way to actualize the conceptual and material aspects of language into awareness and presence. That's a little heavy, perhaps. I basically tried to frame my "poetic" thinking through the more technical and applied elements of the language I work within.

Riprap #2: Sound

"akokli (goat) creek" is a syntactically complex poem, focusing on a proper name. The proper name is a part of language that you focus on in other poems, not least in the collection titled *Breathin' My Name with a Sigh* (which you told me is a line from the 1939 song "Deep Purple"), and including "MHT 55" in this selection.

Akokli is on the east shore of Kootenay Lake in B.C., and the Kootenai language was once spoken across a vast territory (ceded under President James Buchanan), including southern parts of B.C. as well as Montana, Wyoming, Idaho. But now there's apparently under two hundred Ktunaxa speakers. Linguists say that the language is, moreover, unique, like Basque, unrelated to any other. The www.firstvoices.com project is archiving indigenous languages with hopes of revitalizing them, including Ktunaxa.

As a speaker of English, I ask myself: Why is there more music in the word *akokli* than *goat*? There are three times as many singable vowels. To an English-tuned ear, *akokli* already sounds, even without poetic elaboration, like a gurgling creek. I am thinking especially of the liquid consonant [l] that follows immediately after the plosive [k]: two clinking consonants creating a deliciously cold effect. It's the only place in the word where vowel doesn't alternate with consonant.

Akokli is musical in this cultural sense in part because, to someone who doesn't know what the word means, nor any Ktunaxa, the sound-combination seems without a controlling idea. This is very much the way Wallace Stevens approached non-English place and river names of New England, which often were brought into the dominant language and map from aboriginal languages.

The musical spell of the word "akokli" is made pleasing to an English-tuned ear; the poem foregrounds the word's sounds. In contrast, *Breathin' My Name with a Sigh* and "MHT 55" try not to aesthetically induce but rather socially *undo* the sound-spell that has culturally accrued over a proper name sound-sequence within the dominant language.

I had been impressed with Charles Olson's poem "Place; & Names," which was the focus of one of the discussions at the 1963 Vancouver Poetry Conference [http://slought.org/content/11098/]. Here was a notion of history as "cellular" and story as "minute, truthful, and particular." I found permission, in other words, to use the local—*my local*—in poetry, and I began to use poetry as a way to investigate my own particular local, the mountainous region of the West Kootenay. "Naming" became an overtly poetic (and political) act.

Breathin' My Name with a Sigh was a crucial turn for me and the "naming" therein generated most of what I was interested in writing during the '80s. Studying phonology gave me the schwa [ə] and that rippled for me notions of breath, death (my father's), and body alongside my own "racialized" name. I like your sense of "socially" undoing the aesthetics of the proper name. *Breathin'* generated a channel of writing for me that has helped me unpack the cultural weight of hybridity I felt burdened with by the end of the '70s and, by and large, gets worked out in *Diamond Grill*. "MHT 55" plays with, among other texts, the "mistaken" names from mail and get placed here as "difference," that dynamic in language that establishes the distinguishing features of a language (and cultural) event.

During the summer of 1964 I worked for Kootenay Forest Products as a timber cruiser, and the Akokli Creek watershed was one of the cruises we did. My recollected image is that the sign on the highway bridge over the creek read "Akokli (Goat) Creek." I didn't have the facility to check that out then. I probably would have later when I worked on *Pictograms from the Interior of B.C.* But, in hindsight, I think I was attracted to that conjunction of the aboriginal specificity of language and place and early notions of translation, the "trans-" that has become so important to the core of my own thinking around poetry.

Riprap #3: Meaning

Mountain is your second book, from 1967, Canada's centennial. In the second excerpt from *Mountain* included in this selection, eyes are everywhere, except in the mountain itself, which doesn't look back at the perceiver:

> even the eyes a lake is or creek fills
> and the map the eye is a circle makes
> the Mountain isn't.

This excerpt in effect complicates any reading of *Mountain* along the lines that it is "about identifying" with a mountainous place, thereby complicating any reading of Fred Wah as "regional poet": here the lake is an eye (mirror of narcissus), the map is an eye (perceptual pathways to knowledge), but "the mountain isn't" an eye, it doesn't reflect the speaker back upon himself. Place (mountain) doesn't either confirm or deny identity (self).

In 1965, eco-poet Gary Snyder published translations of the T'ang dynasty poet Han-shan for whom remote Cold Mountain, as it was called, was "a house / without beams or walls," on top of which the poet often found his ease, with "No more tangled, hung-up mind." Snyder explains: "When he [Han-shan] talks about Cold Mountain he means himself, his home, his state of mind." Han-shan is the mountain; identification is complete, as Snyder translates it.

By contrast, *Mountain* enacts mountainness, and difference. *Mountain* has little to do with Snyder's sinophilic identifications and thematic treatments. Merely to put them in relation like this is to render them falsely equivalent projects. *Mountain* is not a project engaged with the ancient Chinese poetic tradition—as was the case for many progressive poets since the end of the Second World War and for many eurocentric modernists before them.

> *Mountain* was originally written as a "term paper" for a graduate course I did with Charles Olson in 1964–65. At the time I found it quite difficult to articulate the importance of place and body in how I wanted to approach poetic composition. His essay on proprioception was central and his opening of the long poem as a structure felt new. I don't think I had yet seen Snyder's Cold Mountain poems, though his early poem "Riprap" had made a strong impact on me with its clear sense of "work" in the mountains, work that I had done and felt.
>
> The poetic address I was most interested in at that time was the local and its physical. That, in a large sense, works for most of the writing I did in the '60s and '70s. I was looking for a language to enact the geographical, to align the body with the place; literal sensation of being there, moving through the bush, touch, looking at it all. But the poem itself works with the phenomenal and generates, at least for me, a movement that is open to investigation, surprise, turn. I didn't have anything in mind to say, other than where the language of the poem led me. I think your term "enact" is a desirable one in this context. And of course I see now, underlying this, particularly in a poem like "Mountain," are tendencies of "imagism" and poems like William Carlos Williams's "Desert Music." And I was certainly aware of Pound's "poeia" and, I think particularly in this poem, phanopoeia, that "casting of the image." And, since you mention Snyder's sinophilia, I should admit my own roots here in Ernest Fenellosa's *The Chinese Written Character as a Medium for Poetry*. That is, the composition behind *Mountain* was at least partially

informed by the "ideogrammic" and Pound's notion that the ideogram contains action. "Movement, at any cost," Olson had reminded us.

Riprap #4: Writing Arc

One might juxtapose the natural object represented by the word *tree* with the genetic and familial metaphor *family tree*. In your early writing, the natural object prevails, as does the proprioceptive technique that facilitates "objectism." There's a great and long poetic tradition—and much lore—about the importance of trees for poets that you tap when you turn the word "tree" into a verb, in "Among." Trees also appear sociopolitically in "Hamill's Last Stand" and in many of your other poems.

In your later writing, the genetic and familial metaphor prevails, and the proprioceptive technique that once decentred the *I* (wasn't "anti-humanism" a catchword then?) superseded by a politicized, theorized sense of the *I* as socially constituted and constructed (thus the critique of humanism and of decentring the *I* continues but in such a way as to allow autobiography, diary, and other modes into writing).

Yet both the natural object and the genetic and familial metaphor are juxtaposed in an untitled poem from *Tree* (1972), whose last stanza reads:

> hillsides
> kids or apples
> sap
>   (think of it
> flows

The physical and the local continued as an attention for me during the '70s and the writing of *Tree* was an attempt to tune the local landscape with "community," a term that continues to generate currency. As you say, the trees become sociopolitical. The "I" shifts slightly towards a "We"; "tree" is also "trees." The work, industry, and economics emerge and the local is also social. Notably, the book was published by Vancouver Community Press and it was produced, over one weekend, with the help of the small Quaker community in Argenta, at the north end of Kootenay Lake. "Hamill's Last Stand" was recently republished in *The Purcell Suite: Upholding the Wild*, an anthology of writing aimed at preserving the Purcell Wilderness Conservancy. So, yes, though I see now a kind of subtle transition or widening in my writing into what you call "the genetic and familial," this all gets implicated in the "social" performance of writing as, literally, an act that is shared.

One of the poems included here is "September spawn" from *Pictograms from the Interior of B.C.* That poem literally celebrates community, "cousins and old friends." I must have stumbled on the word "cousins" and I think I've always known what a door that was to the biotextual focus my writing took on in the '80s and '90s. But the '60s and '70s were rife with fresh senses of the "public"; in an attempt to engage with that contemporary I felt most comfortable writing within the concreteness of place.

Riprap #5: Prose

You are perhaps best known today as author of *Diamond Grill*, an autobiography (that you frame as a "biofiction"). I wonder if it may be difficult for some of your readers *not* to resort to *Diamond Grill* as an explanatory framework through which to see your poetry. Imagine the following elision. Aporias in the poetry having to do with issues of poetic form and content may be explained away, with *Diamond Grill*'s unwitting help, as symptoms of a traumatic inability to remember, recognize, act on the poet's family history, but that, now, with this autobiography, the poet has successfully overcome his trauma and accomplished a reconstruction of the missing parts of his past, so that there is no reason to go over these what may then be construed as earlier incomplete "drafts" of his life story. To such readers, couldn't one stress that these poems are not "drafts" of prose?

An example. The lines "one by one one can / become the other" from the pictogrammatic poem beginning "We are different" can be read after *Diamond Grill* as an allegory of racialization, the white self gradually acknowledging its constitutive otherness. But the poem says more than this and says it differently than *Diamond Grill*—and such differences are completely aside from the complex relationships between not only image and text but the paleolithic and the contemporary that these poems evoke. For instance, the interspecies argument of the poem is part of what is unique to the poem and its book, and functions to reflexively situate it in relation to its dominant theme—which is an aboriginal one. The figure of "aboriginality" formally and ideologically mediates and enables the argument of these poems, much as the planet's nonhuman species and life forms themselves mediate between "you or I" in the poem. When you align yourself with aboriginal writers in *Faking It*, it comes from the politics of form inside your own poems such as this one.

The success of *Diamond Grill* has posed an editorial challenge of sorts. I've not included certain poems in this selection because they might too readily serve as representative and exemplary instances of a unified seamless narrative of a poet's writing and life arcs. I've instead chosen poems for their complexity as poems, social and formal acts and addresses, poems that demonstrate technical range of experimentation. I've wanted to emphasize opacities not to detract from the value of establishing a metanarrative from *Diamond Grill* but rather to deepen and complicate that narrative by plunging it into the micro-specifics of particular poem-facts as poem-facts, for which autobiography is only one of many modes from which these poems draw.

As you say, *Diamond Grill* might set up grounds for another kind of reading and you rightly suggest those clues. Considering your selection, however, it might be worth commenting on *Music at the Heart of Thinking* as part of the complex compositional framework I can now respond to with some hindsight. That series, which has really offered itself as some kind of lifelong poem, has a particular dynamic that includes a range of biotextual, geographical, linguistic, literary, physical, and so forth, diction. The words themselves; simply how one word leads to another (not necessarily the next). I've always been interested in poetic composition as an investigative act and I use *MHT* as a site for working out tendencies and ideas. And form. The push towards prose, for me, has been primarily through the prose poem. Williams's *Kora in Hell* has been at my side like a dictionary. Even as early as *Mountain* I've always been fascinated with the generative nature of improvisation. I think the act of writing for me is akin to the jazz trumpet I played as a teenager. That form of phrasing that builds on itself and opens to possibility and iteration. I've always felt that *Diamond Grill*, for example, is the third section of a long poem that includes *Breathin' My Name with a Sigh* and *Waiting for Saskatchewan*. And I'd stress the importance of the serial poem and the long poem behind most of this writing. Perhaps hybridized out of *MHT* and my ongoing fascination with what you call the "natural object" is the utaniki, a form that includes both poetry and prose, and is a biotext, a journal. I use that mix in "Dead in My Tracks: Wildcat Creek Utaniki" as a way to meld a variety of attentions. My point here is that I hope the writing can be read less as intention and more as process.

Thanks for the riprap!

Acknowledgements

Louis Cabri thanks Fred Wah for the generous exchange that begins on page 65, Xu Bing for the cover image, Nicole Markotić for her editorial prowess, Jamelie Hassan for her counsel, and the great team at Laurier Press for the whole package. The editors and the publisher are grateful to those copyright holders who granted permission to reprint previously published work.

From *Mountain* (Buffalo, NY: Audit Press, 1967)
    Mountain that has come over me
    even the eyes

From *Lardeau* (Toronto: Island Press, 1965)
    akokli (goat) creek
    Gold Hill

From *Among* (Toronto: Coach House Press, 1972)
    Among
    Poem for Turning
    For the Western Gate

From *Tree* (Vancouver: Vancouver Community Press, 1972)
    Havoc Nation
    Hamill's Last Stand

From *Earth* (Canton, NY: Institute of Further Studies, 1974)
    Chain

From *Pictograms from the Interior of B.C.* (Vancouver: Talonbooks, 1975)
    September spawn ...
    nv s ble ...

We are different
From *Breathin' My Name with a Sigh* (Vancouver: Talonbooks, 1981)
 sounds of o and ree
 Breathe dust like you breathe wind
 Sigh. A tenuous slight stream
 A hight

From *Waiting For Saskatchewan* (Winnipeg: Turnstone Press, 1985)
 Aug 5

From *Music at the Heart of Thinking* (Red Deer, AB: Red Deer College Press, 1987)
 Music at the Heart of Thinking 1
 Music at the Heart of Thinking 6
 Music at the Heart of Thinking 28
 Music at the Heart of Thinking 50
 Music at the Heart of Thinking 55

From *Alley Alley Home Free* (Red Deer, AB: Red Deer College Press, 1992)
 Music at the Heart of Thinking 77
 Music at the Heart of Thinking 78
 Music at the Heart of Thinking 89
 Music at the Heart of Thinking 93
 Music at the Heart of Thinking 98
 ArtKnot 1
 ArtKnot 2
 ArtKnot 4

From *So Far* (Vancouver: Talonbooks, 1991)
 Hermes Poems
 The Poem Called Syntax
 Dead in My Tracks: Wildcat Creek Utaniki

From *Isadora Blue* (Victoria, BC: La Mano Izquierda Impresora, 2005)
 Hey, Man

From *Sentenced to Light* (Vancouver: Talonbooks, 2008)
 (*sentenced*)

lps Books in the Laurier Poetry Series

Published by Wilfrid Laurier University Press

Don McKay *Field Marks: The Poetry of Don McKay*, edited by Méira Cook,
with an afterword by Don McKay • 2006 • xxvi + 60 pp. •
ISBN-10: 0-88920-494-2; ISBN-13: 978-0-88920-494-2

Al Purdy *The More Easily Kept Illusions: The Poetry of Al Purdy*, edited by
Robert Budde, with an afterword by Russell Brown • 2006 • xvi +
80 pp. • ISBN-10: 0-88920-490-X; ISBN-13: 978-0-88920-490-4

Fred Wah *The False Laws of Narrative: The Poetry of Fred Wah*, edited by Louis
Cabri, with an afterword by Fred Wah • 2009 • xxiv + 78 pp. •
ISBN 978-1-555458-046-0